There's a Rang-Tan in My Bedroom

Written by **James Sellick**

Illustrated by **Frann Preston-Gannon**

wren
&rook

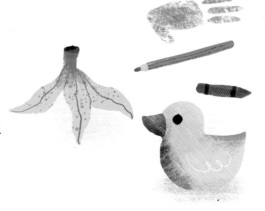

A foreword by
Emma Thompson

The first time I saw an orangutan in real life, I jumped with fright. I heard a great commotion in the trees above me and there he was, swinging through the branches, his huge plate-shaped face staring down at me.

As I stood, rooted to the spot, he came lower to get a better look. His expression was so human-like I felt he could have begun talking at any moment. If he had, I'm quite sure he would have said, "Just look at this place. What have you lot done to my home?"

The rainforest habitat of the orangutan in Indonesia, filled with lush trees and plants reaching high up into the clouds, is being destroyed. In its place, palm trees are being planted.

These palm trees are mainly being grown by big companies to make palm oil, which gets put into stuff we buy like chocolate and shampoo – in fact, there is palm oil in around half the products on our supermarket shelves.

Soon, there will be very little rainforest left for the orangutans. It's not fair.

But we can't just feel sorry for these beautiful creatures. We need to try and make things better for them by speaking up and demanding change. It's time to protect our beautiful planet.

Emma

There's a Rang-tan in my bedroom
and I don't know what to do.

When it comes to basic manners
she just doesn't have a clue.

She plays with all my teddies
and keeps borrowing my shoe.

She climbs up all the plants
and she won't stop shouting

OOOOOOO!

She throws away
my chocolate

and she howls at
my shampoo.

I tried to eat some cookies
and she even stole them too!

There's a Rang-tan in my bedroom
and I don't want her to stay.

So I told the naughty Rang-tan
that she had to

GO AWAY!

Oh Rang-tan in my bedroom, just before you go.

Why WERE you in my bedroom? I really want to know...

There's a human in my forest
and I don't know what to do.

He's destroying all our trees
for your food and your shampoo.

There's a human in my forest
and I don't know what to do.

He took away my family
and I'm scared he'll take me too.

There are humans in my forest
and I don't know what to do.

They're burning it for palm oil...

...so I thought I'd stay with you.

Oh Rang-tan in my bedroom,
now I do know what to do!

I'll fight to save your home
and I'll stop you feeling blue.

I'll share your story
far and wide...

...so others can fight too.

Oh Rang-tan in my bedroom,
I swear it on the stars...

the future's not yet written,
but I'll make sure it is ours.

All About Orangutans

Beautiful orangutans like Rang-tan live on the south-east Asian islands of Borneo and Sumatra. They spend most of their lives in trees in the rainforest – they even sleep in leafy tree nests!

Doesn't Rang-tan look a little bit like you? That's because orangutans are one of the closest relatives to humans. In fact, the word "orangutan" is from the Malay language – "orang" means human and "utan" comes from a word meaning forest. So orangutan means "human of the forest"!

But we're not doing a very good job of looking after our ape cousins. Sadly, there are only about 110,000 orangutans left in the world. That's because their rainforest homes are being destroyed to make way for palm oil plantations.

The Problem with Palm Oil

Humans use a lot of palm oil — you can find it in lots of things your family buys at the supermarket, from chocolate, crisps and cookies to toothpaste, shampoo and soap.

Palm oil comes from the fruits of palm trees. There is nothing wrong with palm oil if it's grown responsibly, without chopping down the rainforests.

But the problem is that a lot of palm oil ISNT grown responsibly. Instead, tropical rainforests are being torn down so that more and more palm trees can be planted. Animals like orangutans, elephants and tigers are losing their homes.

HOW YOU CAN HELP

If you want to help protect animals like Rang-tan, and the local people who live in the forests, here are three things you can do.

Tell all of your friends!

Share Rang-tan's story with as many of your friends and family as possible. Tell everyone you know about the problem with palm oil, and the way it harms animals.

Tell some other people too.

Making a poster to put up in your area is a great way to let lots of other people know about Rang-tan. Ask your library or a local shop to display it for you.

BIG CHOCOLATE COMPANY BOSS
BIG CHOCOLATE COMPANY
CHOCOLATE TOWN

ME
MY HOUSE
MY TOWN

DEAR BIG CHOCOLATE COMPANY BOSS

YOURS SINCERELY
ME

Write a letter to companies that use palm oil, asking them to save the rainforests.

If everyone asks the maker of their favourite chocolate bar or shampoo to stop buying palm oil from companies destroying the rainforests, they'll really sit up and take notice. Ask a grown-up to find the company's address online (it's often on their website if you click on "Contact Us"). Turn the page to find out how to write a great campaign letter.

TOP TIPS
for writing a
campaign letter!

① Keep your letter short so it's easy and quick to read.

② Make it personal – tell them why you care about the rainforests, so they understand why it's so important.

③ Stay positive – tell them how they can feel good about saving the rainforests.

④ Why not draw a picture to make your letter stand out?

⑤ Don't forget to include your address on the letter so they can send you a reply.